STANDING IN THE

PERFECT STORM

By Dennis Paul Goldsworthy-Davis

Open Wells Ministries

15315 Capital Port

Sam Antonio, TX 78249

www.openwellsministries.org

Foreword by Amy Rylander

Library of Congress Number:

ISBN: 978-1-7355716-2-1

Printed in the United States of America
by Open Wells Ministries International

ACKNOWLEDGEMENTS

I would like to thank my first pastor Bennie Finch, although he has passed on a few years ago, he first taught me how to take a stand in prayer and in the word. Alan Vincent, was also a great influence on me and stood in the midst of many a conflict. My own father, whom I never saw back down to anything or anyone, clearly influenced my life and helped create the attitude that would stand in God. All of these were great father figures, thank God for each one...

I would like to thank Jeannie Hartman for her help in so many ways. What a blessing to the body of Christ!

Lastly my loving wife, who alongside the Holy Spirit, would challenge me in every moment of weakness...

DEDICATION

I would like to dedicate this book to the memories of so many that affected my life. Those who helped shape me. Bennie Finch, Robert Fairnie, Alan Vincent and Bob Maine.

To my wife who has stood by me for all these years and my spiritual son, Chris Rodes, who has constantly spurred me on.

OTHER BOOKS
BY DENNIS PAUL GOLDSWORTHY-DAVIS

Unlimited Anointings

The God of Jacob

Grace Looks Good on You

Walking in The Prophetic

TABLE OF CONTENTS

FOREWORD

I have had the pleasure of knowing Dennis and experiencing his ministry for over 10 years now. His faithfulness and dedication to see the body of Christ walk in her fullness and destiny is inspiring. I have never met anyone that carries such a tangible anointing that literally brings people into encounters with God. The passion he has causes those that meet him to hunger to know and experience more of God.

God is a dreamer and a promise giver. He has dreams and plans for each one of us. The beauty of the prophetic is that it allows us to have a glimpse into God's dreams for us. The prophetic causes us to know why God created us and what the Lord desires for our lives. The reality of prophecy, however, is that not every prophetic word is a guarantee. The Lord desires every human-being first to know Him and have a relationship with Him, and He also wants every person to fulfill every purpose for which He created them. God is all about relationship and fellowship with His creation. He wants us to walk out His plans for our lives with His help and guidance. He longs to co-labor with us and bring heaven to earth together.

The more I come to know God, the more I realize there are no shortcuts in the kingdom. We live in a fast-paced world of drive-thrus and instant access. However, the kingdom is steadily advancing just like a seed progressively growing into a fruit bearing tree. It doesn't happen overnight and neither does most of our callings and promises.

In 2010, I had a near death experience where the enemy tried to kill me. As I laid there in the hospital bleeding out, something in my spirit rose up and I realized I was not finished on this earth yet. I had so many promises from God that had not yet come to pass. I instantly knew in my heart that I was NOT going to die yet! I laid there in that hospital emergency room and stood upon the promises that God had already given me. Suddenly, the peace of God came to me and I had absolutely no fear. I walked out of that hospital the next day and began walking towards my destiny.

There are many different reasons for the delay in our promises. Some of those things are God and some are not. We live in a fallen world and there is a very real enemy that hates you and does not want you to accomplish the plans God has for you. Satan wants to kill, steal and destroy you and your dreams. We must learn how to war with our promises and stand firm in all circumstances.

> "Finally, be strong in the Lord and in the strength of His might. Put on the full armor of God, so that you will be able to stand firm against the schemes of the devil. Therefore, take up the full armor of God, so that you will be able to resist in the evil day, and having done everything, to stand firm." Ephesians 6:10-11,13 NASB1995

Sometimes our promises are delayed not because of the enemy, but because the Lord is still growing and maturing us so that we are ready to walk in our promises. Just like that fruit tree, we must endure the process of maturing to bear the desired fruit.

"Therefore, having been justified by faith, we have peace with God through our Lord Jesus Christ, through whom also we have obtained our introduction by faith into this grace in which we stand; and we exult in hope of the glory of God. And not only this, but we also exult in our tribulations, knowing that tribulation brings about perseverance; and perseverance, proven character; and proven character, hope; and hope does not disappoint, because the love of God has been poured out within our hearts through the Holy Spirit who was given to us."

Romans 5:1-5 NASB1995

Every good tree produces good fruit. According to the scriptures, with God we can do all things, but apart from Him we can do nothing (nothing of eternal value). Everything we do that is kingdom will be fruit bearing. If we abide in Jesus, we will produce eternal fruit.

"Abide in Me, and I in you. As the branch cannot bear fruit of itself unless it abides in the vine, so neither can you unless you abide in Me. I am the vine, you are the branches; he who abides in Me and I in him, he bears much fruit, for apart from Me you can do nothing. You did not choose Me but I chose you, and appointed you that you would go and bear fruit, and that your fruit would remain, so that whatever you ask of the Father in My name He may give to you." John 15:4-5, 16 NASB1995

Ezekiel 47 describes the River of God which is the Holy Spirit flowing from the throne of God. The Lord desires for us to be trees that are planted by the River and produce fruit in every season of our lives. Whether you are in a dry wilderness season, a stormy sea season, or in a glorious harvest season, we should be bearing fruit in our lives and steadily walking towards our promises.

> "By the river on its bank, on one side and on the other, will grow all kinds of trees for food. Their leaves will not wither and their fruit will not fail. They will bear every month because their water flows from the sanctuary, and their fruit will be for food and their leaves for healing.""
>
> Ezekiel 47:12 NASB1995

Dennis has weathered many storms and has produced lasting kingdom fruit through it all. He has gained wisdom and revelation that will encourage and equip you to persevere in the midst of the fires of life. My prayer is that as you read this book you will receive an impartation and a divine tenacity that will help you face every battle. I also pray that you obtain every tool required to successfully walk out your calling and purpose until every promise God has given you is manifested. Attitude is everything. The promises of God are "Yes" and "Amen", but we must be willing to make sacrifices and face the storms of life and press on towards the high calling of God.

Amy Rylander

Founder, We Are One Activation Center

Prophetic Artist, Amy Rylander Art

Author, *Unlocked*

INTRODUCTION

Even those who are not avid movie goers will
remember the movie that was called *The Perfect
Storm*. It was based on a true story and featured the
actor, George Clooney. It was about three raging
weather fronts that collided in 1991. Quite a movie
and quite a story. But the words *perfect storm* could
be used again and again regarding our lives. Jesus
warned of the storms that come against our houses or
lives:

> *"But the one who hears my words and does
> not put them into practice is like a man who
> built a house on the ground without a
> foundation. The moment the torrent struck
> that house, it collapsed and its destruction
> was complete."* Luke 6:49

He warned that they would come but often we are
unprepared and without knowledge of the actual
warfare that we are involved in. In the book of Hosea
we are told by the prophet quite clearly,

> *"My people are destroyed by a lack of
> knowledge."* Hosea 4:6

So, interesting that this very Chapter begins with,
"Hear the word of the Lord". The Bible is given to
enable us to gain knowledge. The Holy Spirit is given
to reveal knowledge. God ministers to teach
knowledge. Quite impressive if we are those who
want to gain knowledge.

So, what is our perfect storm? It is the storm that has been released against us personally. In Ephesians once again we are clearly warned that we are in a battle against spiritual forces in various realms.

> *"We wrestle not against flesh and blood."*
> Ephesians 6:12

Verse 11 clearly outlines who is behind it!

> *"The devil's schemes." Ephesians 6:11*

The word *schemes* means *craftiness, trickery* and *wiles*. It includes *travesty* and *deceit*. These are his methods against you. The perfect storm aimed at you.

The purpose of this booklet is to make us aware of the reasons for these storms and some of the methods used against us and to show us how to overcome. Our call is to *"STAND!"*. Knowing such things can help us in our stand. We can become like Paul who said,

> "We are not ignorant of his devices."
> 2 Corinthians 2:11

But also, like Paul, we can become

> "Strong in the Lord." Ephesians 6:10

I had wanted to entitle this booklet *What the Hell?* because, indeed, what we wrestle with comes from the hellish one. I decided against the title, not wanting the enemy to get an occasion through offense or misunderstanding. Just one more scheme.

STANDING FOR YOUR FAITH

When Paul tells us three times to stand in Ephesians Chapter 6, it is clear what the enemy is after: what we stand for, what we stand on and to take away our fight.

We need to know the purpose of his schemes and trickery as well as his methods.

He is after our faith! The first recorded attack of the enemy is found in Genesis. Chapter 3 makes the clear statement,

> *"The serpent was more crafty than any of the wild animals God had made."* Genesis 3:1

Wow! There it is, right at the beginning…more crafty, more full of schemes and wiles and deception.

His method of attack? "Has God said?" Did he really say? Did he really mean that? His attack was on the person and the words of God. His purpose is to take away our faith. If I can't trust who God is I can't then trust what God says. Or alternatively, if I can't trust what God says how can I trust who he is? His method is to cast a dispersion, cause us to doubt. The next moment we are no longer standing in our faith. "He can't have meant that because..." "His promise sure seems to be a long time coming." "Maybe he has favorites and didn't mean me." And so it goes on.

He is after our walk with God! Consider God coming to the garden and saying,

> *"Adam, where are you?"* Genesis 3:9

Just eight verses later, there it is. Adam now has stopped walking with God. Therein lies the second scheme. Cast a dispersion and now we feel because we messed up we can't walk with God anymore. "I can't walk with a God I don't trust. Equally my failure is so glaring. I am naked. I am ashamed. I failed, so I must hide."

Our walk with God is our privilege as a son of God but the enemy wants to separate us, alienate us from the fellowship that the Lord procured for us. The Song of Solomon covers it so beautifully.

> *"My dove in the clefts of the rock, in the hiding places on the mountainside, show me your face, let me hear your voice; for your voice is sweet, and your face is lovely."* Song of Solomon 2:14

The Lord is saying, "Let me see your face and hear your voice".

He describes her face and voice but her answer is, "It's the foxes, they ruined the vineyard." We get so caught up in what is wrong that we don't fellowship anymore but rather turn our face away and stop our communication. His very communication shows his heart toward us. He looks for Adam in the garden, "Adam, where are you?" He wants fellowship but the enemy has brought a separation.

He is after our identity! We saw clearly the attack against the first Adam which is representative of the attack on mankind. But now here comes the attack on the last Adam. "If you are…I challenge your identity." But it goes further,

> *"If you are the son of God."* Matthew 4:3

In other words, "Prove who you are but I throw doubt in it.". But here comes the third part. "Prove it to me! Satan. Fall into my trap of putting God to the test."

This is the same attack that is leveled at all that are in Christ. Because he is after Christ's identity, he is after our identity in him. Challenging who we are in God, challenging our sonship and challenging our inheritance. If he can get us to doubt it, we will never step into our fullness as a son and our inheritance that we share in Christ. He wants us to stay in a slave mentality instead of a son mentality. He wants us to doubt God's purpose for us and in us and to ultimately make us lame and unfruitful. Jesus had none of it and neither should we.

He is after our stance!

> *"Stand firm..."* Ephesians 6:14

That means be unmovable and unshakable. The enemy is after our stance in Christ, not only doubting ourselves and God but losing our footing so that we slip. He wants to get us off the rock into the sand as in Luke 6:48-49. He wants to get us to become feeble and slip off the path as in Hebrews 12:12-13. Feeble knees stop praying. Feet that cannot stand cannot race or fight. Years ago, I studied Karate and one of the most important lessons was the stance. It was important to master so that we could not be easily knocked over. Hebrews 12 also warns us of several other things that will affect our footing: In verse 1, sin that entangles alongside false burdens and then weariness. In verse 2, eyes away from the master and on other things. All are intended to take away our footing.

He is after our anointings! One of the most precious things given by God alongside salvation is the anointings by his Spirit. The enemy hates them! Why? They are a devil defeater.

> *"...how God anointed Jesus of Nazareth with the Holy Spirit and power, and how he went around doing good and healing all who were under the power of the devil..."* Acts 10:38

The anointings we have are devil defeating and God exalting. The enemy wants us to give them up or not use them or lose trust in them so to weaken our effectiveness in this life. This is such a large subject that the book, *Unlimited Anointings*, covers some of the realms these anointings can operate in.

He is after our promise and our hope! Listen again to the words that were used in the Garden, "Has God said?". He is after our promise from God. If he can get us to let go then we won't stand on our promise. We will let our promise go. First comes dispersion and then comes the heart growing faint, or sickly.

> *"Hope deferred makes the heart sick..."* Proverbs 13:12

Along then comes hopelessness. If he can steal our promise and hope, he can steal our future. Pointlessness and lack of purpose comes in which often leads to backsliding.

He wants to devour and destroy us! Peter warns us in his writings so categorically of what the enemy is up to. This is the Peter (Simon, as he was known originally) that Jesus told of the schemes against him.

> *"Simon, Simon, behold, Satan hath desired to have you, that he may sift you as wheat."*
> Luke 22:31 KJV.

Thank God, Jesus followed this statement with a wonderful revelation!

> *"But I have prayed for thee, that thy faith fail not."*
> Luke 22:32 KJV

Again, he went after his faith by sifting him. Now read what Peter says:

> *"Be sober, be vigilant; because your adversary the devil, as a roaring lion, walketh about seeking whom he may devour."* 1 Peter 5:8 KJV

The word *devour* means *to destroy, swallow up and drown.* He wants to destroy and drown our faith and walk.

How amazing that in Peter's case, as in Job's, he asks permission!

He wants to hinder you! Several times in the New Testament, Paul speaks of being hindered.

> *"For we wanted to come to you-certainly I, Paul, did again and again-but Satan blocked our way."*
> 1 Thessalonians 2:18

The word *blocked* here means *to impede* and *detain and cut into…to stop our purpose* and ministry, using every method at his disposal.

These are just a few of his purposes. Clearly his main

objective is to stop the work of God and destroy any that work those works or have faith in him.

LEARNING THE METHODS
USED AGAINST US

Paul writing to the Corinthians makes this statement:

> *"...Lest Satan get an advantage against us, for we are not ignorant of his devices."*
> 2 Corinthians 2:12 NIV

Paul had learned many of his methods and so wanted to help the church gain an understanding. I personally love his statement, *"Lest Satan get an advantage"*. He didn't say win. He meant the intention was to momentarily get an upper hand and a seeming victory! The ultimate winning is ours because,

> "Greater is he that is in us" 1 John 1:4

Also, Romans so clearly states,

> *"No, in all these things we are more than conquerors through him who loved us."*
> Romans 8:37

We must remember that we are not just dealing with schemes and plans and methods here on earth but also in heavenly places.

"For our struggle is not against flesh and blood, but against the rulers, against the authorities, against the powers of this dark world and against the spiritual forces of evil in the heavenly realms." Ephesians 6:12

He wars above and wars below. Alan Vincent, a great man of God and mentor to me, so aptly stated in his writings that he is a legalist and so, as in the case of Job, he tried to use even God to render judgement. Because he wars above and below, understanding some of the methods he uses before we talk about our stand is absolutely important to us.

The Method of Legal Wrangling! In both the cases of Peter and Job, the enemy asked for a right to attack. Of course, I do realize that in both cases it was before the blood of Jesus was shed, but we read in Revelation,

> *".... for the accuser of our brothers and sisters, who accuses them before our God day and night, has been hurled down."* Revelation 12:10

We are being accused both day and night by the accuser himself. This is after the blood is shed. But, of course, as we will learn later it is the blood that is one of our defense systems.

We are also told,

> *"...But if anybody does sin, we have an advocate with the Father-Jesus Christ, the Righteous One."* 1 John 2:1

Surely the blood should speak for itself. Yes and, YES! But he is also an advocate against accusations released against us in heavenly places or courts. The enemy tries to use legality against us with a righteous God. He accuses using sins and bloodlines. The sins of the fathers to the bloodline of multiple generations is first mentioned in Exodus:

> *"...he punishes the children and their children for the sin of the parents to the third and fourth generation."* Exodus 34: 7

In the case of Peter an accusation was cast against an action of pride and Job also questioned the fairness of God. He also loves to use the curses of those who are in authority, the curse of a parent over you or a curse of the bloodline and words used against you. And so it goes on.

The Method of Doubt! Again, going back to the first crafty attack of the serpent, here it is: *let's throw a little doubt in here.* Doubt God, doubt his word, doubt yourself, doubt your calling and your promise and soon you're doubting if you are saved and doubt the intentions of others and so it goes on. You're soon doubting the veracity of scripture and so forth. He goes first to the heavens and now he is going to your head itself to works his schemes. He tried to even get Jesus to doubt he was the son of God, maybe he has tried that with you. Doubt your anointing and doubt you received the Holy Spirit. This scheme must be shown and overthrown. Remember, he is a liar and he is the author of negativism.

The Method of Buffeting! Paul speaks of this in 2 Corinthians 12 Verses 7-10.

> *"Therefore, in order to keep me from becoming conceited, I was given a thorn in my flesh, a messenger of Satan, to torment me."*
> 2 Corinthians 12:7

This passage is mind blowing if grasped. Paul is attacked by a messenger of Satan who is buffeting him. The word *buffet* basically means *to punch continually*. It's like you are in the ring but you never asked to step in. Hit after hit, blow after blow and strike after strike. You feel like you can't get your head together and can't come up for breath. "What did I do?", you cry! You didn't "do". It's who you are. The aim is to make you ineffective. Make you so caught up in defense that you have no attack left. Paul almost fell for it until the Lord gave him the answer. Go on and throw in the towel? But we have a great scripture,

> *"Though, I walk through the valley of the shadow of death, I will fear no evil...."* Psalms 23:4

We are told he is with us! We are also told we pass through the valley of Baka (the place of weeping).

> *"As they pass through the Valley of Baka, they make it a place of springs...."* Psalm 84:6

These valleys feel like they last forever but indeed they do not. We might feel punch-drunk but this is indeed just a scheme that releases the hand of God.

The Method of Storms! Jesus warns us in the parable of the house built on the rock in Luke 6:46-49: Whether wise or foolish, storms come against us. Better to be wise and build ourselves on the premise of his word! Storms came even against Jesus while asleep in the boat, as the story is told in Mark 4:35-39. The disciples found out that storms came against them not only when he was in the boat but when he wasn't.

But what do these storms look like? Lashing waves and strong winds with rain and thunder and lightning are some of the signs of a storm. Even hail can be added, trying to scare and knock down everything we have built…trying to damage the roof and the windows. How do I know I am in a storm? Because it has more than one element to it. It is powerful and loud! The natural man cannot withstand such things. One needs protection! Ever heard the statement, "It came at us from ever side."? That can be the storm. The perfect storm however, as in the movie, is when several storm systems collide. Paul himself went through a tumultuous storm in the story told in Acts 27. It eventually cost the very ship they were on. As I started to write this, the hurricane Dorian was heading for the Florida coast where I had been ministering for several days.

We must remember that Jesus walked on water in storms and slept through them. But we must also remember that, even walking toward Jesus, Peter looked at the storm and began to sink. Let's be real! They are hard not to look at.

The Method of Missiles! In Ephesians we are warned to protect ourselves:

> *"Above all, taking the shield of faith, wherewith ye shall be able to quench all the fiery darts of the wicked."* Ephesians 6:16 KJV

Fiery darts are actually *flaming arrows* in other versions of the Bible, but it means *directed missiles that are afire* coming at us looking for weak spots. Catching us unaware. This is not the only place such missiles are talked about. Multiple times in the Psalms David speaks of such things. It can come direct or from men but with the same intent to wound and disable! To kill the life within you. To knock the breath out of you. Remember Achilles? This type of attack went for his one uncovered place and finished him. According to Psalm 91, if we hide in God we are covered. But the enemy looks for that moment and even tries when we stand in God.

> *"You will not fear the terror of night, nor the arrow that flies by day...it will not come near you."*
> Psalm 91:5, 7

Clearly, according to Ephesians 6, it goes after our faith or where we are weak in faith or where there is no shield. One of the words for *fiery* is *angry*...coming against us with anger burning to wound and damage.

Have you ever made the statement, "It just came out of the blue!!", meaning you weren't expecting that? Or another statement, "It was like a shot in the dark"? Such is the intent of these arrows. Who sees an arrow coming? Once again, there is an armament given by God to defend us that we will look into in another chapter.

The Method of Loneliness and Separation! I will never forget the advice given me when I was a youth pastor. I was young and was wanting to enter fully into the call of God on my life. A slightly older man than I had just come from a few years as an independent ministry in a pioneer situation. He was clearly battered by his attempt to serve God. This was his advice: "Dennis, don't let the enemy separate you from the brotherhood of the local church by persuading you to go it alone." He went on, "He will separate you and then work to pick you off." This guy knew firsthand! Great advice!!

Now look at when Satan attacked Jesus while he was alone in the wilderness! Notice, he's alone and in comes the enemy. This was Jesus! If it was done to Jesus you can imagine that it will be aimed at us, too. We have been added to a body, to church accountability and to relationships but if we can be persuaded to go it alone then the enemy can seek to pick us off.

What would make us want to draw aside and be alone? Some suggestions follow:

Deception. Tricked into thinking we are called into this or sometimes even being "led" to take another job that has more pay but no fellowship connected or to pioneer on our own.

Offenses. The very word means *to fall away*.

Loss of trust in others. It makes us make unwise decisions.

Separation. When under trial we often separate ourselves.

Self pity. Speaks for itself.

And the list can go on.

The Method of Betrayal! I will call this the Judas factor. Judas was the one who ate with Jesus but betrayed him for money. Betrayal can cause a massive wound! Normally, to betray one has to be close. Absalom did it to David and he was a son. Moses had more than one leader do it to him. Paul spoke of it by name. It may be betrayal in ministry or betrayal in relationships. The betrayal of broken promises. Adultery is another form of betrayal. In all the cases we see in the Bible so often the enemy is involved at the inception and in the result. In the case of Judas, the Bible even says that Satan entered his heart!

> *"As soon as Judas took the bread, Satan entered into him."* John 13:27

The arch betrayer will use betrayal as his tool. I have watched firsthand the power of betrayal on a person and have experienced it multiple times. Its wounds can be so severe that folks can be crippled in their walk. Often betrayed folks become suicidal.

The Method of Being Tricked into Pride! This was the downfall of the enemy himself. Isaiah 14 covers this in a shocking revelation. Pride makes one think they are more than they are. Ezekiel 28 tells the story of the king of Tyre. The king of pride sure knows how to wield this one. I have always felt that three things will test you greatly. Success, position and promotion. Of course, one must consider the tests of anointing, wealth and the accolades of others. Listen to this scripture that proves this point!

> *"Not being a novice, Lest being lifted up with pride, he will fall into the condemnation of the devil."*
> 1 Timothy 3:6 KJV

The danger with pride is that it exalts itself above its ability to stand. Such was the enemy's sin. If you can be tricked into pride you find yourself to be exclusive, arrogant and separated from accountability.

The worst issue with pride is that it causes God himself to resist you.

> *"In the same way, you who are younger, submit yourselves to your elders. All of you, clothe yourselves with humility toward one another, because 'God opposes the proud but shows favor to the humble.'"*. 1 Peter 5:5

Many other passages address pride. The clear answer is found in *accountability:* Accountability of elders and brothers and spouses and other gifted ministry. This will help stop this most insidious of attacks.

The Lord dealt with me many years ago as a young prophet in this matter. I was shocked when he revealed it to me. I would have sworn that I was humble. Gosh, there is the evidence! I thought I was humble. Surely my circumstances vouched for that. No friend, to be in humble circumstances does not dictate a humble heart. Listen to the words of the prophet to Saul.

> *"You were once small in your own eyes."*
> 1 Samuel 15:17

That was before he got anointing and power and position! We indeed must watch out for this terribly insidious attack.

The Method of Grief Over Loss! Is there any blow like this blow? Especially when unexpected! What an occasion for the enemy. Jacob so reacted to loss that he refused to be comforted and condemned himself to a life of grief.

"All his sons and daughters came to comfort him, but he refused to be comforted. 'No', he said, 'I will continue to mourn until I join my son in the grave.' So his father wept for him." Genesis 37:35

Look at his reaction! Separation, self-pity and vows to grieve for the rest of his life. Jesus came to turn grief and despair into a place of victory.

"He has sent me....to proclaim the year of the Lord's favor and the day of vengeance of our God, to comfort all who mourn ..." Isaiah 61:2

If we succumb to this attack at such an integral moment of needing both the Lord and others, the attack of loneliness and separation alongside grief and despair can be wielded against us.

Undealt with grief can affect our health quite shockingly. It affects our health, emotions, sleep and eyesight. It can turn into bitterness, resentment and other things. It can even take the body into adrenal shock. Harvard themselves have written papers on such things. All suffer grief in many forms because we live in this life but when the enemy jumps on it the results can be devastating. Thank God he has the antidote through Jesus and his body.

The Method of Self-Pity! The basis of this attack is to have one concentrate on self. It is based on the "poor me" syndrome. It can spring from any of the above-mentioned issues. But to be tricked into feeling sorry for oneself can open the door to such a foothold of the enemy. Self-pity will never dwell alone. It has a sinister root of inverted pride and can often separate or want revenge or can be self-destructive and suicidal. All eyes on self! No eyes on Jesus and who cares about anyone else. Self-pity takes no prisoners and yet it is its own prison. The antidote is quite simple. "All eyes on Jesus!", Shouts the platoon Sargent.

Elijah is perhaps our best example of this terrible sin.

> *"What are you doing here Elijah?"*
> 1 Kings 19:13 NIV

Now look at his pity-answer in verse 14 in the KJV:

> *"...because the children of Israel have forsaken thy covenant, thrown down thine altars, and slain thy prophets with the sword; and I, even I only, am left..."* 1 Kings 19:14 KJV

Gosh, you can't get more "poor me" than that. It caused him to go into depression, run away, judge his ancestors and want to die and then go the wrong way. Where was it from? An attack from Jezebel, Satan's pawn against the prophetic. Who would have known that he who walked with God could fall so far? Lessons to watch and learn my friends. Nobody can pretend they are immune. But we can be aware!

THE ATTITUDE THAT ENABLES US TO STAND

Gaining the Right Attitude

Whatever we go through in our walk and lives and whatever the storm there is always an antidote! The great scripture in 1 Corinthians makes the statement,

> *"But when you are tempted, (put on trial or tested or put under adversity), he will also provide a way out so that you can endure it."* 1 Corinthians 10:13

There is always a way out or through, or an ability to weather it!

Before we examine some of our methods to stand, we need to gain something of an attitude, a mindset, a gaze as it were! All athletes prepare mentally and all those that fight in the ring do so, too. Whatever the skirmish we must be armed with the right attitude. In Ephesians 6, as previously mentioned, we are told three times to STAND! But perhaps there is one verse within those verses that gives us the attitude we need.

"And after you have done everything, to stand, stand...." Ephesians 6:13-14

We must gain an attitude, *"I AM GOING TO STAND!"*. That's the end of the argument. Stand is what I am told and stand I will. Once we gain this attitude, then our ability to stand changes.

A wonderful example of this truth is found in one of the stories of David's mighty men. The man is called Shammah.

> *"But Shammah took his stand in the middle of the field. He defended it and struck the Philistines down, and the Lord brought about a great victory."*
> 2 Samuel 23:12

Victory in the Attitude to Stand

So, the victory lies in the fact that we take our stand. Taking our stand comes from an attitude that says, "I am going to!" and "I will stand!". Having been in a few skirmishes in my life, particularly in the past, when someone has an attitude that they are going to stand up to something often their assailants will back down. When the enemy sees that we won't back down it makes this one who is seeking whom he can devour to realize this is no easy skirmish and often will change the game, as it were.

We are told that we are to have the mind of Christ in Philippians 2:5, and in Isaiah he sets his face as a flint!

*"Because the Sovereign Lord helps me, I will not be
disgraced. Therefore have I set my face like flint,
and I know I will not be put to shame."* Isaiah 50:7

He was armed with the right attitude. If anyone won the
skirmish he did, forever changing the history of man.

There are two great scriptures translated in the NIV version
concerning this:

> *"to be made new in the attitude of your minds."*
> Ephesians 4:23

This surely is the renewing of the mind mentioned in
Romans 12. It is no doubt the work of God but also our
work as we join him in this change of attitude! I will stand!
Yes, I will!

We are also told to arm ourselves with the same attitude as
Christ.

> *"Therefore, since Christ suffered in his body, arm
> yourselves also with the same attitude, because
> whoever suffers in the body is done with sin."*
> 1 Peter 4:1

It seems before we look at our full armament to be used we
need to arm our minds. We will never go beyond our
attitude and our decisions.

Let's say it together! "I will stand, because I can do all things through Christ who strengthens me, therefore I will stand because he will help me stand."

CONSIDERING OUR BASE

Jesus gives a revelation of our fight in Luke 6:46-49, the famous passage about where your house is built. The revelation is twofold; firstly, that storms come to all! To the wise and to the unwise. To the followers and to the non-followers. To those who listen to his word and those who don't! To those who do his word or those who don't. Secondly, the greater revelation in this is what base have we set or placed in our lives on which to stand? Are we rock people or sand people?

Sand people are either not word people at all or those who listen but don't apply what they hear. Those who are entertained by the word, excited by the word but never dig it into their lives and apply it. The revelation sadly continues here, that there is no base on which to stand. For these folks the storm can be a life devastation, crashing all that had been built and leaving our lives in a place of having to rebuild or lean totally on the grace and faith of others to help us through.

Rock people, however, are spoken of differently. Jesus says of them that they not only call him Lord but listen to what he says. But they go further. They put his words into practice! Digging them deep into their lives and making them their stand.

> *"They are like a man building a house, who dug down deep and laid the foundation on rock. When a flood came, the torrent struck that house but could not shake it, because it was well built."* Luke 6:48

The storm, though it still rages, still beats against them, it cannot shift their stand because they become one with the rock himself. How do we become one? It is our application of the word and our relationship with the giver.

So, whether sand or rock, storms are for real. When the base is correct we can stand and, having done all to stand, we will stand! We all love the scripture from John:

> *"Then you will know the truth and the truth will set you free."* John 8:32

But so few ask why the word *then* is at the beginning of this great statement? *Then* is the word that enjoins two statements! It is the verse before which gives us the key:

> *"If you hold to my teaching, you are really my disciples. Then you will know the truth..."* John 8:31

There it is again. The base of all discipleship is the doing and the base of gaining truth is the doing. If we get the base right, we get to stand and fight!

STAND FIRM THEN

What Happens When We Stand

Two scriptures in the Old Testament give a great revelation of what happens when we stand.

> *"But Shammah took his stand in the middle of the field. He defended it and struck the Philistines down and the Lord brought about a great victory."* 2 Samuel 23:12

> *"Next to him was Eleazar son of Dodai the Ahohite, one of the three mighty warriors."* 1 Chronicles 11:12

Both are speaking of one of David's mighty men, Shammah. But what happens when he does stand is enlightening. It is imperative for us to take hold of the fact that Shammah took his stand and because he did, the Lord brought about a great victory. If we stand we release God to move. If we don't, it is not that he can't, but it surely won't be through us. We don't become who he says we can be as promised in Romans.

> *"…more than conquerors through him that loved us"*, Romans 8:37

Encouragements to Stand

I love stumbling upon great scriptures! It's not that we haven't read it before but suddenly it becomes a word of the Lord to us. Here it is!

> *"Now it is God who makes both us and you stand firm in Christ, he anointed us,"* 2 Corinthians 1:21

It is not only God's intention to help us stand but it is his intention to enable us to stand. In fact, speaking of his servants he makes the statement,

> *"He is able to make us stand."* Romans 14:4

He has the ability and the desire but let's catch from some of his methods.

It's all in the context of this great statement, plus a few other great scriptures.

He is Able to Make Us Stand in Christ! Basically, he places us in Christ and that releases the life of Christ in us. His victory, his Spirit, his inheritance, etc.

> *"Christ in you the hope of glory."* Colossians 1:27

He is Able to Make Us Stand by Anointing Us! He anoints us both with the Spirit of Christ but also as a seal or deposit, as it tells us in the next verse,

> *",set his seal of ownership on us, and put his Spirit in our hearts as a deposit, guaranteeing what is to come. "* 2 Corinthians 1:22

He anoints us also with the ministry of the Holy Spirit. This ministry would take another book to explain but Jesus told us so clearly,

> *"And I will ask the Father, and he will give you another advocate to help you and be with you forever... "* John 14:16

He speaks of the Paraclete himself. The one drawn alongside to help and comfort and counsel and strengthen.

He Has Given Us Faith to Stand!

> *"Not that we lord it over your faith, but we work with you for your joy, because it is by faith you stand firm. "* 2 Corinthians 1:24

> *"In addition to all this, take up the shield of faith, with which you can extinguish all the flaming arrows of the evil one. "* Ephesians 6:16

Remember the Bible says that *faith comes* which means *he gave it*.

> *"Faith comes from hearing the message, and the message is heard through the word about Christ. "* Romans 10:17

We receive it and can stand because of our faith in him. Abraham was able to stand by faith in him in Romans Chapter 4.

He has given us promises:

> *"For no matter how many promises God has made, they are 'Yes' in Christ. And so through him the "Amen" is spoken by us to the glory of God."*
> 2 Corinthians 1:20

It was the promise that made Abraham stand. His promises to us do the same whether by scripture, by dreams and visions or by the prophetic. The promises are there to help us stand whatever we face. The old hymn says it well: "Standing on the promises of Christ my King!".

He Has Given Us Preachers and Ministers to Help Us Stand!

> *"For the Son of God, Jesus Christ, who was preached among you by us-by me and Silas and Timothy-was not 'Yes' and 'No', but in him it has always been 'Yes'.* 2 Corinthians 1:19

Christ and truth were preached by Paul, Silvanus and Timothy. Preachers are given by God for the helping of the saints as they reveal the truth, which is our *belt* which we will discuss in the next chapter:

"Stand firm then, with the belt of truth buckled around your waist..." Ephesians 6:14

He Has Given Us Grace to Stand! Grace came with Jesus and it is given more and more as needed it tells us in John1:14-17. There is a throne of Grace in Hebrews:

> *"Let us then approach God's throne of grace with confidence, so that we may receive mercy and find grace to help us in our time of need."* Hebrews 4:16

There is enough grace for whatever we need in 2 Corinthians 12:9-10. In fact, it becomes our sufficiency.

> *"But he said to me, 'My grace is sufficient for you, for my power is made perfect in weakness.'."* 2 Corinthians 12:9

He Has Given Us the Ministry of Encouragement to Stand! He uses both the saints, prophesy, scriptures and so many other tools in the ministry of encouragement!

> *"But encourage one another daily as long as it is called 'Today', so that none of you may be hardened by sin's deceitfulness."* Hebrews 3:13

> *"Anyone who speaks in a tongue edifies themselves, but the one who prophesies edifies the church."* 1 Corinthians 14:4

"For everything that was written in the past was written to teach us, so that through the endurance taught in the Scriptures and the encouragement they provide we might have hope." Romans 15:4

He Has Given Us the Prayers of the Saints to Help Us Stand! God uses the saints to bring deliverance as they war on our behalf. Who knows how many times we have been brought through as others have prayed for us? This stands out:

> *"...On him we have set our hope that he will continue to deliver us as you help us by your prayers."* 2 Corinthians 1:10-11

How Do We Take Our Stand

Once we know that the Lord is able to make us stand and help us the attitude to stand springs forth in our being, but what methods can we use? What is out our disposal? All the above things mentioned! What does that mean? We can stand in Christ, the anointing, the promises and the grace mentioned above and in all that God has given.

With those tools in hand we must then be strong in the Lord. Developing a strong relationship, a strong trust and a strong faith in the Lord is key.

> *"Finally, be strong in the Lord and in his mighty power."* Ephesians 6:10

We can't be a weekend Christian or special days Christian. We must be a Christian who walks with his God. Like Noah and Enoch in Genesis Chapter 5 and 6, we must be strong in his word and in relationship with the Holy Spirit. This thought could grow into its own book:

> *"...but the people that do know their God shall be strong, and do exploits."* Daniel 11:32 KJV

Strength to stand also comes in knowing the power of God experientially, being baptized in the Holy Spirit and conversant with the Spirit and his ways.

> *"And be not drunk with wine, wherein is excess; but be filled with the Spirit;"* Ephesians 5:18 KJV

It's hard to defeat a Spirit filled man! There is a great prayer that I want us to know!

> *"I pray that the eyes of your heart may be enlightened in order that you may know the hope to which he has called you, the riches of his glorious inheritance in his holy people and his incomparably great power for us who believe. That power is the same as the mighty strength..."* Ephesians 1:18-19

Know what is available in the power of God for you! Know how the power of God works on our behalf and what makes Gods power move on behalf of his children and saints. Great truth and awesome in battle!

Understanding the Armor of God

It is so important to understand our armor found in Ephesians 6: 14-18.

The Belt of Truth means knowing the truth himself and the truth of the Word and what God says in any matter.

> *"Jesus answered, 'I am the way and the truth and the life. No one comes to the Father except through me.'."* John 14:6

> *"Sanctify them by the truth; your word is truth."* John 17:17

Why the belt? Because it touches our inner man. Remember, "out of your belly flows"....our inner man covered by truth.

The Breastplate of Righteousness really means having our heart sanctified, purified and kept right with God and man. The enemy has no ground if my heart is right.

> *"Above all else keep you heart, for out of it are the issues of life."* Proverbs 4:23

A heart kept right is hard to cause to grow faint or give up in times of storm.

The Helmet of Salvation simply means cover your head with God's thinking, God's word and thoughts touched by the blood. We are told to keep our eyes on Jesus and set our affections on things above. We must have a thinking that is covered by the things of God...not circumstantial or negative.

> *"...fixing our eyes on Jesus, the pioneer and perfecter of faith..."* Hebrews 12:2

> *"Set your minds on things above, not on earthly things."* Colossians 3:2

Feet That are Shod with the Preparation of the Gospel of Peace means don't just talk it, walk it! Carry it and manifest it. Carry the good news and walk in the Spirit; hard to knock a man down like that. To walk in peace means I live in peace, manifest peace and walk in peace with others and myself. The accuser of the brethren can't accuse one too easily who lives like that.

The Shield of Faith is another subject for a book all on its own. It is using our faith and the confession of our faith to deflect and stop fiery darts or arrows. It was Abraham's faith in God's word and ability that enabled him to stand. "Has God said?", the enemy asks. Yes, he has! I have read it and heard it and know he can and will do it. The spirit of faith has to do with believing and confession.

> *"It is written: 'I believed; therefore I have spoken.' Since we have that same spirit of faith, we also believe and therefore speak..."* 2 Corinthians 4:13

If I *believe*, it is hard to rob me but if I *confess* it, WOW, now I deflect your attack! One of the greatest confessions of a saint that I love to use is found in Psalms:

> *"I would have fainted, unless I had believed to see the goodness of God in the land of the living."*
> Psalms 27:13

It is an awesome confession that I know who God is and how he acts! But I know it is for me! It's hard to beat down a faith like that. I believe it is a good habit to state often what we believe and what has been promised.

The sword of the Spirit, which is the word of God. There is no better example than that of Jesus while attacked by Satan. "IT IS WRITTEN!...", Jesus exclaimed! Self-explanatory. Do it like Jesus did and you get the same results. I will never forget the story of John Wesley. When attacked by a highwayman he shouted a scripture out that haunted his attacker. Years later he met him in a marketplace and the man was born again because of the sword that John had used: "The blood of Jesus Christ, God's son cleanses from all sin." He used the powerful word of God which even the enemy has no power over.

Praying in the Spirit

This means letting the Holy Spirit pray through you and enabling you to pray. Praying in tongues cannot be ignored here. It is his language, especially when we have nothing to say. The Bible says it builds us up:

"Anyone who speaks in a tongue edifies themselves…" 1 Corinthians 14:4

Praying in the Spirit also prays in accordance with the will of God and alongside the one who ever lives to intercede for us. Great habit to get into, when not in a storm, so that in a storm that's just what you do!

Dealing With the Accuser of the Brethren

How do we do that? Well quite simply, we quote and stand in what the lamb did in his blood.

> *"Then I heard a loud voice in heaven say: 'Now have come the salvation and the power and the kingdom of our God, and the authority of his Messiah. For the accuser of our brothers and sisters, who accuses them before our God day and night, has been hurled down.'"* Revelation 12:10

The enemy cannot cross that! Washed in the blood is washed in the blood. But even more than that, the blood is to be used on your behalf. I remember an old friend praying it out loud over his wife and she was miraculously healed. We are blood bought and blood washed and that blood never loses its power.

Next, in the same verse we never let go of our testimony. It releases the blood and the Holy Spirit into action. A great example of this is found in Zechariah 3. The accuser was attacking Joshua, the high priest, before the angel of the Lord and the answer was powerful:

> *"The Lord said to Satan, 'The Lord rebuke you, Satan! The Lord, who has chosen Jerusalem, rebuke you! Is not this man a burning stick snatched from the fire?'"* Zechariah 3:2

That's what happens when we stand in the work of the cross and our testimony!

We have come to God, the righteous judge. We have a right to plead our case in his court. We have a right for justice and a ruling on behalf of his children. The blood testifies and so do we!

> *"[But you have come] to the church of the firstborn, whose names are written in heaven. You have come to God, the Judge of all, to the spirits of the righteous made perfect, to Jesus the mediator of a new covenant, and to the sprinkled blood that speaks a better word than the blood of Abel."* Hebrews 12:23-24

Let's learn to operate on our behalf in his courts! There are, of course, some great books on the subject.

Let's arm ourselves with the knowledge that God is able to make us stand. Let's get an attitude we will stand and then use his divine methods to stand!

Calling Into Remembrance

This is what David did when he found himself in quite a place in Psalm 63. He is driven from the sanctuary he loves and out in the wilderness with the enemy clearly hounding him and wanting to kill him. Right in the middle of it is something he does that is a fascinating tool of defense. He calls into remembrance. He remembers the Lord himself in verse 6 and what God had done in verse 2. He remembers God's love in Verse 3. This, my friends, is a tremendous weapon. Remind yourself of who he is, what he has done and what he has promised. Remember his salvation as Peter says:

> *"But whoever does not have [these qualities] is nearsighted and blind, forgetting that they have been cleansed from their past sins."* 2 Peter 1:9

Folks, remembering what he has done will stir up your faith and enable you to stand! It is not long before David starts prophesying and chasing God afresh. Psalm 63 itself is so refreshing and strengthening when we are seeking to stand.

Self Encouragement

David is once more in a tough place in 1 Samuel 30. His home has been ransacked, wives and children stolen and his men are thinking of stoning him. It doesn't get much rougher than that! He wept and wept but suddenly found strength.

"David was greatly distressed...but David found strength in the Lord his God." 1 Samuel 30:6

When we start to encourage ourselves it releases that great strength of God which is itself dynamic. We use memory of promises, past victories and our belief system. We stir up old prophesies and new. We speak our own encouragement out, even when they are no others to encourage us. We become, by the Holy Spirit, our own support system.

I believe that perhaps we should make this a practice of our lives so that when in a storm and all is hurled at us we can overflow from this strong foundation that we have built.

TESTIMONIAL

"You need encouragement, just like we all do. We live in difficult times. While God is doing amazing things, he is also shaking the heavens and the earth as Scripture warns. This perfect storm comes upon us, at times, from every side. Dennis, who is always good in the Word of God, here again in this book, gives us a solidly Biblical description of how to be strengthened to stay standing in the storm. It's a very helpful read".

Dr. Barry Wissler
President

HarvestNet International
We Fulfill the Great Commission Together

BIOGRAPHY

Dennis Paul Goldsworthy-Davis has been blessed to travel extensively throughout the world ministering both apostolically and prophetically to the body of Christ. He operates within a strong governmental prophetic office and frequently sees the Presence of God and the Spirit of Revival break out upon the lives of people. Dennis has equally been graced to relate to many spiritual sons throughout the earth, bringing wisdom, guidance and encouragement.

Born in Southern Ireland and raised in England, Dennis was radically saved from a life of drugs and violence in 1973. Soon after his conversion, he began to operate within his local church where he was fathered spiritually by Bennie Finch, a seasoned apostolic minister. After working in youth ministry Dennis pastored in several areas within the U.K. It was during these pastorates that Dennis began to see profound moves of God in these same venues.

In 1986 Dennis experienced a dramatic shift in his life and ministry. He and his family moved to San Antonio, Texas, to join a vibrant, functioning apostolic team.
In 1990 Dennis was commissioned to start Great Grace International Christian Center, a local work in San Antonio. Dennis continues to serve as the Senior /Minister of GGICC and heads the formation of the apostolic team in the local house. Presently, Dennis relates to several functioning apostolic ministries. He draws wisdom and accountability from Robert Henderson of Global

Reformers, Barry Wissler of HarvestNet International and for many years before his passing, Alan Vincent. Each of these carry strong, well-seasoned apostolic offices in their own right.

Dennis has been married to his wife Christine since 1973 and has two wonderful daughters and four grandchildren.